Poptropica® English Islands

TEST BOOKLET 2

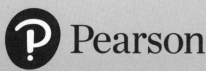

Pearson

Contents

Introduction

Evaluation can be described as an attempt to analyse the learning that a pupil has achieved over a period of time as a result of the classroom teaching/learning situation. It plays an integral part in the teaching and learning process.

The evaluation material in this Test Booklet has been designed to analyse pupils' progress, with the aim of reinforcing the positive aspects and identifying areas for improvement.

There are five main reasons for evaluation:

Formative – to increase motivation by making evaluation a part of the continuous learning process.

Summative – to give pupils feedback on their progress or achievement at a particular point in time, often formally through tests.

Informative – to give pupils and parents feedback on progress or achievements.

Diagnostic – to monitor individual pupils' needs and help identify pupils who need special support.

Evaluative – to identify pupils' level of achievement and select or order pupils according to merit, to check effectiveness of teaching methods, teaching materials and teachers.

This Test Booklet contains one Placement test, eight Unit tests, three End of term tests, one Final test, and one Exam preparation test.

The Placement test can be used as a diagnostic test at the start of the year, reviewing learning from the previous year and helping to assess pupils' ability.

The Unit tests can be used at the end of each unit, to monitor pupils' progress through the course, to give pupils feedback on their achievement and to identify areas requiring reinforcement.

The End of term and Final tests can be used as informative and evaluative tests, for reporting purposes.

The Exam preparation test can be used to help prepare pupils for external exams such as CYLETS and Trinity.

A and B versions have been provided for the Unit tests, the Final test and the Exam preparation test. Both versions cover exactly the same learning objectives, and will provide an equal level of evaluation. You may find it useful to hand out different A and B versions to students who sit next to each other. Alternatively, you could use the A version to test the whole class and use the B version for reinforcement purposes.

The four skills of Reading, Writing, Listening and Speaking are tested through self-explanatory activities that students will be familiar with from their work in class.

Each activity has its own score, with a consolidated score at the end of each page and a total score at the end of each test. Points have been allocated according to the number of tasks pupils are required to do in each activity.

For Speaking activities, points have been allocated according to the learning objectives. In the lower levels of the course, points should be awarded for correct word identification. In the higher levels of the course, longer answers are expected, and points should be awarded for production of the target language. Pupils should be allowed to make more than one attempt, and you should encourage them to self-correct.

Preparation for evaluation

Procedure on the day before the evaluation

- Review unit content using games to give practice for the coming evaluation.
- Ask pupils to predict what they think the content of the evaluation might be, using L1 as needed.

Procedure on the day of evaluation

- Play a game, and sing a song or chant to help pupils to move from L1 to English.
- Play the audio and direct pupils to complete the listening activities. Audio files are available on the Active Teach, or at pearsonelt.com/islands.
- As with the audio throughout this course, you may wish to pause the audio to allow pupils to complete each question.
- Depending on your classroom setup, you may wish to set pupils up in pairs to complete the speaking activity and monitor the class as a whole. Alternatively, you may prefer to have pupils speak individually to you while the remainder of the class works through the reading and writing exercises.
- Have some small pieces of scrap paper available for students to make notes for their speaking evaluation. Emphasise that they only should make notes. Try to avoid full sentences or scripts being written.
- Set pupils a time limit within which to complete the remainder of the test.
- Pupils will need colouring pens or pencils for some of the activities.
- Check the answers against the Answer Key on pages 72–75. Please note that the answers for the speaking activities are intended as suggested answers only. Write the total score in the space provided at the bottom of each page and at the end of the tests.
- When handing tests back to pupils, go through the answers and explain any errors.

Poptropica English Islands also encourages the practice of self-evaluation, which is provided at the end of each unit in the Activity Book. This gives the pupils an important opportunity to express their own opinion about their progress in English.

1 Read and circle. Then match. (12 points)

1 What's (this / these)?

2 Where ('s / are) my uncle?

3 What's (you / your) favourite colour?

4 (Has / Have) she got long hair?

5 (Are / Is) it big?

6 (Does / Do) you like fish?

a Yes, she has.

b No, I don't.

c It's a rubber.

d No, it isn't. It's small.

e It's green.

f He's in the living room.

2 Read and write the letter. Then colour. (12 points)

1 a red boat ☐

2 a small brown house ☐

3 a green frog ☐

4 three yellow bananas ☐

5 a blue shirt ☐

6 two grey clouds ☐

a **b** **c** **d** **e** **f**

3 Read and match. (6 points)

1 thirty

2 twenty-seven

3 fifty

4 forty-three

5 thirty-nine

6 twenty

43

20

39

27

50

30

Score: _____ /30

1 **Read and write. (6 points)**

| are   haven't   would   's   Have   's |

1 What _____ that?

2 What _____ those?

3 _____ you got a parrot?

4 No, I _____ got a parrot.

5 What _____ you like?

6 Where _____ Tony?

2 **Read and answer. (6 points)**

1 What's your favourite colour?

_____

2 Have you got a hamster?

_____

3 Do you like vegetables?

_____

4 Are you hungry?

_____

5 Can you touch your toes?

_____

6 When's your birthday?

_____

3 **Look and write. (8 points)**

| big/small/long/short
one/two/four
eyes/ears/legs/tail |

1 It's _____.

2 It's got _____.

3 It's got _____.

4 It's got _____.

Score: ____ /20

1  **Listen and match. (10 points)**

1 10		green	cars
2 15		blue	kites
3 12		yellow	bikes
4 19		purple	boats
5 14		brown	trains

2 **Listen and ✓. (8 points)**

five ☐   house ☐   uncle ☐   blue ☐   dog ☐

garden ☐   twelve ☐   green ☐   car ☐   bike ☐

3 **Listen and write the missing letters. (6 points)**

1 e _ _ _ _ _ _

2 b _ _ _ _

3 y _ _ _ _ _ _

4 k _ _ _ _

5 k _ _ _ _ _ _ _

6 p _ _ _ _ _

4 **Look and say. (6 points)**

What's this?   It's …   It's got …

Score: ___ /30

Whole test score: ___ /80

1 **Read and circle. Then match. (8 points)**

1 What are (this / these)?
2 What's (those / that)?
3 What's your favourite (colour / colours)?
4 How many (bike / bikes) are there?

a There are six.
b They're dolls.
c It's a red ball.
d Blue.

2 **Read and write the letter. Then colour. (12 points)**

1 What's that? It's a yellow car. ☐
2 What are those? They're balls. There are six green balls. ☐
3 How many kites are there? There are five blue kites. ☐
4 What's that? It's the number twenty-nine. It's black. ☐
5 What's this? It's a brown lorry. ☐
6 How many dolls are there? There are three purple dolls. ☐

3 **Read and write. (4 points)**

| toys   motorbike   twenty   these |

1 How many _____ are there?
2 There are _____ toys.
3 What are _____?
4 It's a black _____.

4 **Draw your favourite toy and write. (6 points)**

This is my favourite toy.

1 What is it?

_____

_____

2 What colour is it?

_____

_____

Score: ____ /30

My toys

1 **Listen and write *True* or *False*. (5 points)**

1 Sam's birthday is in October. _____

2 Paula's favourite month is July. _____

3 Jimmy's got three favourite colours. _____

4 Sarah's favourite day is Saturday. _____

5 Barry's favourite colour is brown. _____

2 **Listen and match. Then write. (6 points)**

1 Charlie   **a** presents _____

2 Sue   **b** boat ___1___

3 Harry   **c** kites _____

4 Helen   **d** toys _____

3 **Listen and number. Then colour. (8 points)**

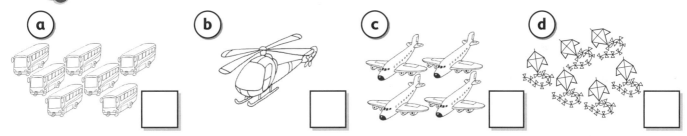

a   **b**   **c**   **d**

4 **Look and say. (6 points)**

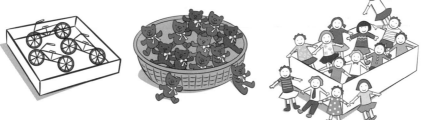

How many ... are there?   What's this?   What are these?

Score: ____ /25

Whole test score: ____ /55

1 Read and circle. Then match. (8 points)

1 What's (that / those)?
2 What are (those / that)?
3 What's your favourite (colours / colour)?
4 How many (kite / kites) are there?

a They're teddy bears.
b There are eight.
c It's a purple boat.
d Green.

2 Read and write the letter. Then colour. (12 points)

1 What's this? It's a black and white ball. ☐
2 What are those? They're yellow kites. There are five kites. ☐
3 How many helicopters are there? There are two grey helicopters. ☐
4 What's that? It's the number thirty-seven. It's blue and red. ☐
5 What's this? It's a red bus. ☐
6 How many blue boats are there? There are three. ☐

a   b   c   d   37   e   f

3 Read and write. (4 points)

bikes   those   lorry   fifty

1 There are _____ dolls.
2 What are _____?
3 How many _____ are there?
4 It's a yellow _____.

4 Draw your favourite toy and write. (6 points)

This is my favourite toy.

1 What is it?

_____

_____

2 What colour is it?

_____

_____

Score: ___ /30

1 **Listen and write *True* or *False*. (5 points)**

1 Sam's birthday is in August. _____

2 Paula's favourite month is June. _____

3 Jimmy's favourite colours are blue and white. _____

4 Sarah's favourite day is Sunday. _____

5 Barry's favourite colour is red. _____

2 **Listen and match. Then write. (6 points)**

1 Charlie		**a**	toys	_____
2 Sue		**b**	boat	1
3 Harry		**c**	presents	_____
4 Helen		**d**	kites	_____

3 **Listen and number. Then colour. (8 points)**

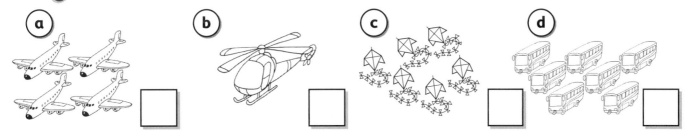

4 **Look and say. (6 points)**

How many ... are there?   What's this?   What are these?

Score: _____ /25

Whole test score: _____ /55

1 **Read and match. (4 points)**

1 Who's he?
2 Who's she?
3 Where's your aunt?
4 Where's your uncle?

a She's my aunt.
b He's in the kitchen.
c He's my cousin.
d She's in the bedroom.

2 **Read. Then look and write the letter. (5 points)**

1 My granny is in the bathroom. ☐
2 My son is in the living room. ☐
3 My grandad is in the kitchen. ☐
4 My uncle is in the attic. ☐
5 My cousins are in the bedroom. ☐

a b c d e

3 **Read and write. (5 points)**

cousin   kitchen   parents   bedrooms   house

1 This is my _____.
2 There are three _____.
3 My grandad is in the _____.
4 My _____ is in the bathroom.
5 My _____ are in the living room.

4 **Draw your family and write. (6 points)**

This is my family.

1 How many children are there?

_____

2 How many cousins have you got?

_____

3 What are your parents' names?

_____

Score: ____ /20

1 Listen and write the number. (4 points)

Kim

1 _____ uncle(s)
2 _____ aunt(s)
3 _____ cousin(s)
4 _____ brother(s)

2 Listen and match. (5 points)

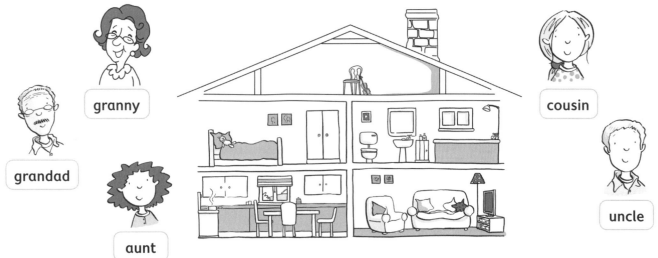

granny

grandad

aunt

cousin

uncle

3 Draw your house and say. (6 points)

How many ... are there?

Where's/Where are ...?

Score: ____ /15

Whole test score: ____ /35

1 **Read and match. (4 points)**

1 Where's your daughter?   a He's my grandad.
2 Who's she?   b She's in the attic.
3 Who's he?   c He's in the hall.
4 Where's your son?   d She's my granny.

2 **Read. Then look and write the letter. (5 points)**

1 My two cousins are in the flat.   ☐
2 My grandad is in the living room.   ☐
3 My daughter is in the hall.   ☐
4 My sons are in the house.   ☐
5 My uncle is in the attic.   ☐

a   **b**   **c**   **d**   **e**

3 **Read and write. (5 points)**

| bathrooms   living room   grandparents   aunt   flat |

1 This is my _____.
2 There are two _____.
3 My _____ are in the kitchen.
4 My uncle is in the _____.
5 My _____ is in the bedroom.

4 **Draw your house and write. (6 points)**

This is my house.

1 Is it big/small?

_____

2 How many bedrooms are there?

_____

3 What's in the living room?

_____

Score: ___ /20

2 My family

1 **Listen and write the number. (4 points)**

Andy

1 _____ uncle(s)

2 _____ aunt(s)

3 _____ cousin(s)

4 _____ sister(s)

2 **Listen and match. (5 points)**

uncle

granny

grandad

cousin

aunt

3 **Draw your family and say. (6 points)**

Who's he/she?

Who are they?

Score: _____ /15

Whole test score: _____ /35

1 Read and match. (4 points)

1	nod your	**a**	fingers
2	shake your	**b**	body
3	point your	**c**	head
4	touch your	**d**	toes

2 Read. Then look and write the letter. (4 points)

1 I can do cartwheels. ☐

2 I can swim. ☐

3 I can climb. ☐

4 I can stand on my head. ☐

a **b** **c** **d**

3 Write. (4 points)

1 (climb?) (you) (Can) _____

2 (you) (swim?) (Can) _____

3 (you) (a) (ball?) (catch) (Can) _____

4 (you) (do) (Can) (cartwheels?) _____

4 Draw what you can and can't do. Then write. (8 points)

Activities

1 I can _____.

2 I can _____.

3 I can't _____.

4 I can't _____.

Score: ____ /20

1 Listen and number. (6 points)

a  ☐

b  ☐

c  ☐

d  ☐

e  ☐

f  ☐

 2 Listen and ✓ or ✗. (8 points)

	climb	swim	do the splits	stand on your head
Bob				
Mel				

3 Complete for yourself and ✓. Then say. (6 points)

	can	can't
swim		
stand on my head		
climb		
do the splits		
move my legs		

Can you ...?

I can/can't ...

Score: ___ /20

Whole test score: ___ /40

1 **Read and match. (4 points)**

1 move your
2 wave your
3 clap your
4 point your

a fingers
b legs
c hands
d arms

2 **Read. Then look and write the letter. (4 points)**

1 I can throw a ball. ☐
2 I can do the splits. ☐
3 I can touch my toes. ☐
4 I can catch a ball. ☐

a **b**  **c**  **d**

3 **Write. (4 points)**

1 do you splits? Can the _____
2 you Can skip? _____
3 touch your toes? Can you _____
4 you swing? Can _____

4 **Draw what your friend can and can't do. Then write. (8 points)**

Activities
1 He/She can _____.
2 He/She can _____.
3 He/She can't _____.
4 He/She can't _____.

Score: ___ /20

1 Listen and number. **(6 points)**

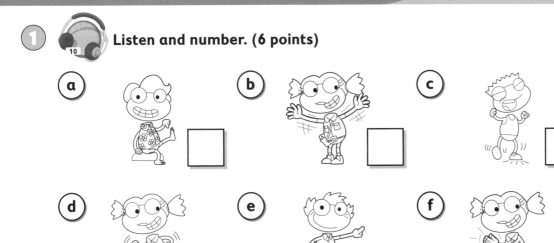

a ☐ b ☐ c ☐

d ☐ e ☐ f ☐

2 Listen and ✓ or ✗. **(8 points)**

	climb	swim	do the splits	stand on your head
Mel				
Bob				

3 Complete for yourself and ✓. Then say. **(6 points)**

	can	can't
touch my toes		
wave my arms		
throw a ball		
clap my hands		
shake my body		

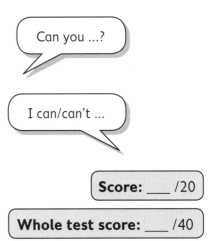

Can you ...?

I can/can't ...

Score: ____ /20

Whole test score: ____ /40

1 **Read and match. (4 points)**

1 Have you got long hair?	**a** No, he hasn't. He's got small ears.
2 Have you got a small mouth?	**b** No, I haven't. I've got short hair.
3 Has she got blue eyes?	**c** Yes, she has.
4 Has he got big ears?	**d** Yes, I have.

2 **Read. Then look and match. (6 points)**

1 Kate's hair is long and straight.
2 James' hair is short and curly.
3 Emma's got short, neat hair.
4 Sue's got long, messy hair.
5 Tim's got short, neat hair.
6 Toby's got short, messy hair.

3 **Write. (4 points)**

1 ears? you small got Have _____

2 you got dark Have short, hair? _____

3 you brown Have eyes? got _____

4 hair? straight you Have long, got _____

4 **Draw your face and write. (6 points)**

This is me.

I've got _____ eyes.

I've got _____

_____.

I haven't got _____

_____.

Score: ____ /20

1 **Listen and write *True* or *False*. (8 points)**

Gemma

1 She's got a small face. _____

2 She's got a pink nose. _____

3 Her eyes are green. _____

4 Her ears are big. _____

Brian

5 His hair is brown. _____

6 He's got a big mouth. _____

7 His nose is big. _____

8 He's got a big face. _____

2 **Listen and ✓. (6 points)**

	long	short	straight	curly	neat	messy
Dorothy						
Mick						

3 **Draw your friend's face and say. (6 points)**

Has he/she got ...?

He's/She's got ...

He/she hasn't got ...

Score: ____ /20

Whole test score: ____ /40

1 **Read and match. (4 points)**

1   Has she got messy hair?
2   Have you got a small mouth?
3   Has he got dark hair?
4   Have you got brown eyes?

a   Yes, I have.
b   Yes, he has.
c   No, she hasn't. She's got neat hair.
d   No, I haven't. I've got green eyes.

2 **Read. Then look and match. (6 points)**

1   Tim's got short, neat hair.
2   Kate's hair is long and straight.
3   Toby's got short, messy hair.
4   Jame's hair is short and curly.
5   Sue's got long, messy hair.
6   Emma's got short, neat hair.

3 **Write. (4 points)**

1   got   long,   Have   straight   you   hair?   _____

2   blue   Have   you   eyes?   got   _____

3   hair?   got   Have   messy   you   _____

4   short,   you   got   Have   curly   hair?   _____

4 **Draw your friend's face and write. (6 points)**

This is my friend.

My friend's got _____ eyes.

He's/She's got _____

_____.

He/She hasn't got _____

_____.

Score: ____ /20

1 **Listen and write *True* or *False*. (8 points)**

Gemma

1 She hasn't got a small face. _____

2 Her nose is red. _____

3 She's got blue eyes. _____

4 Her ears aren't big. _____

Brian

5 His ears are small. _____

6 His eyes are brown. _____

7 He hasn't got a big nose. _____

8 He's got a small face. _____

2 **Listen and ✓. (6 points)**

	short	long	curly	straight	messy	neat
Dorothy						
Mick						

3 **Draw your face and say. (6 points)**

Have you got ...?

I've got ...

I haven't got ...

Score: ____ /20

Whole test score: ____ /40

1 **Read and match. (3 points)**

1 It's white.
It's got four legs and a short tail.

2 It's got two legs and two wings.
It can swim.

3 It's got a long tail.
It's got long hair on the head.
It can run fast.

a horse

b duck

c sheep

2 **Read. Then look and match. (6 points)**

1 What's this? It's a bat.
2 What are these? They're ducks.
3 What are those? They're owls.
4 What's that? It's a goat.
5 What's that? It's a hen.
6 What's this? It's a lizard.

a

b

c

d

e

f

3 **Write. (5 points)**

1 big? Are the hens

2 white? the goats Are

3 the ducks Are long?

4 black? the bats Are

5 Are foxes? they

_____

_____

_____

_____

_____

4 **Draw bats and write. (6 points)**

These are bats.

Are they big? _____

What can they do? _____

Have they got wings? _____

Score: ____ /20

© Pearson Education Limited 2017 PHOTOCOPIABLE

1 Listen and number. (5 points)

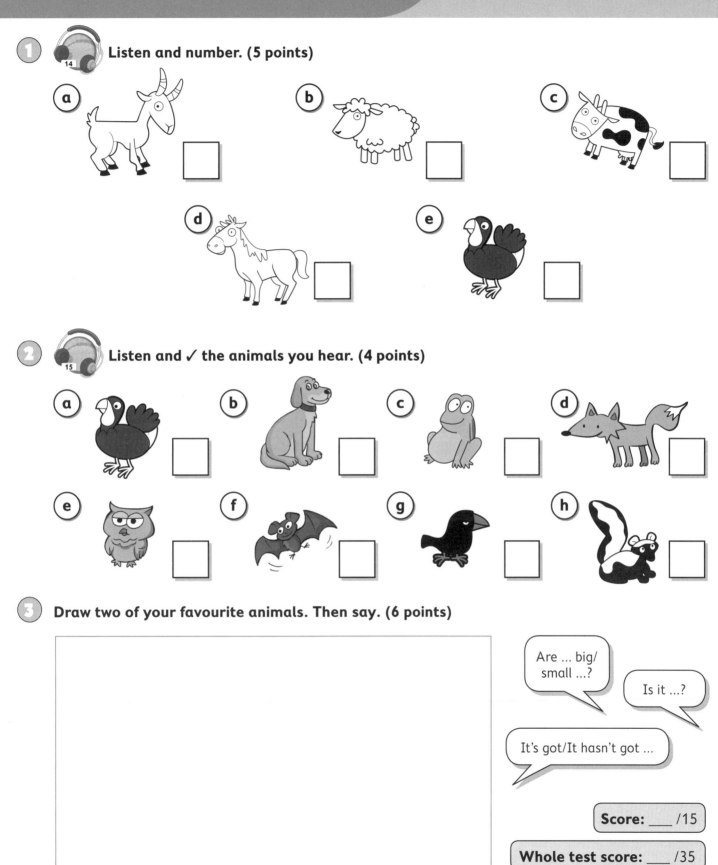

a

b

c

d

e

2 Listen and ✓ the animals you hear. (4 points)

a   b   c   d

e   f   g   h

3 Draw two of your favourite animals. Then say. (6 points)

Are ... big/ small ...?

Is it ...?

It's got/It hasn't got ...

Score: ___ /15

Whole test score: ___ /35

1 Read and match. (3 points)

1 It's small and brown.
   It's got two wings.

2 It's big and it's got a long, thin tail.
   It hasn't got hair on the head.
   It can't run fast.

3 It's got two legs and two wings.
   It's got a tail.
   It isn't a hen and it isn't a duck!

a hen

b turkey

c cow

2 Read. Then look and match. (6 points)

1 What's that? It's a goat.
2 What are those? They're skunks.
3 What are these? They're owls.
4 What's this? It's a hen.
5 What's that? It's a frog.
6 What's this? It's a bat.

a   b   c

d   e   f

3 Write. (5 points)

1 small? Are the hens

2 white? Are the bats

3 the lizards short? Are

4 Are foxes? they

5 the goats Are white?

_____

_____

_____

_____

_____

4 Draw bats and write. (6 points)

These are bats. What colour are bats?

They're _____.

Are they big or small? _____

Are they awake in the day or at night?

_____

Score: ____ /20

1 🎧 14 **Listen and number. (5 points)**

a [ ]　　b [ ]　　c [ ]

d [ ]　　e [ ]

2 🎧 15 **Listen and ✓ the animals you hear. (4 points)**

a [ ]　　b [ ]　　c [ ]　　d [ ]

e [ ]　　f [ ]　　g [ ]　　h [ ]

3 **Draw two of your favourite animals. Then say. (6 points)**

Are ... big/ small ...?

Is it ...?

It's got/It hasn't got ...

Score: ___ /15

Whole test score: ___ /35

1 **Find and write. Then draw. (4 points)**

1 salpep _____

2 otsat _____

3 gseg _____

4 azipz _____

2 **Look. Then circle and write. (8 points)**

1

2

✓

3

✓

4

✗

1 I (like / don't like) _____.

3 I (like / don't like) _____.

2 I (like / don't like) _____.

4 I (like / don't like) _____.

3 **Write. (5 points)**

1 pasta? there any Is

_____

2 there beans? any Are

_____

3 some are bananas. There

_____

4 like you Do sweetcorn?

_____

5 toast? like Harry Does

_____

4 **Draw your favourite food and write. (8 points)**

This is my favourite food.

It's _____.

What colour is it? _____

Do you like it for breakfast? _____

What do you like for lunch?

_____

Score: ____ /25

1 Listen and ✓. (8 points)

1 He likes ...

pizza ☐
eggs ☐
cheese ☐
cereal ☐
salad ☐
bananas ☐

2 He doesn't like ...

fish ☐
bread ☐
apples ☐
toast ☐
rice ☐
chicken ☐

2 Listen and ✓ or ✗. (6 points)

Sally						

3 Draw your breakfast, lunch and dinner. Then say. (6 points)

Is/Are there any ...?

There's/There are ... some ...

There isn't/ aren't any ...

Score: ____ /20

Whole test score: ____ /45

1 **Find and write. Then draw. (4 points)**

1 cekinhc _____

2 dasla _____

3 crie _____

4 rrbegus _____

2 **Look. Then circle and write. (8 points)**

① ② ③ ④

✓ ✓ ✗ ✗

1 I (like / don't like) _____.

2 I (like / don't like) _____.

3 I (like / don't like) _____.

4 I (like / don't like) _____.

3 **Write. (5 points)**

1 there) Is) salad?) any) _____

2 any) grapes?) Are) there) _____

3 Helen) like) Does) cereal?) _____

4 you) like) fish?) Do) _____

5 are) apples.) There) some) _____

4 **Draw your breakfast, lunch and dinner. Then write. (8 points)**

These are my breakfast, lunch and dinner.

At breakfast, I eat _____.

At lunch, I _____.

At dinner, _____.

What's your favourite food?

It's _____.

Score: ____ /25

1 🎧 16 **Listen and ✓. (8 points)**

1 | He likes ...

eggs ☐
pizza ☐
cheese ☐
salad ☐
cereal ☐
bananas ☐

2 | He doesn't like ...

bread ☐
fish ☐
toast ☐
apples ☐
rice ☐
chicken ☐

2 🎧 17 **Listen and ✓ or ✗. (6 points)**

Laurence						

3 **Draw the food in your fridge. Then say. (6 points)**

Is/Are there any ...?

There's/There are ... some ...

There isn't/ aren't any ...

Score: ___ /20

Whole test score: ___ /45

1 Write. (5 points)

1 trousers. wearing I'm _____

2 wearing a not T-shirt. I'm _____

3 wearing hat? Are a you _____

4 you wearing? are What _____

5 pink I'm wearing skirt. a _____

2 Read and write the letter. Then colour. (8 points)

1 I'm wearing brown boots. ☐

2 I'm wearing a blue shirt. ☐

3 I'm wearing yellow pyjamas. ☐

4 I'm wearing a green jumper. ☐

a   b   c   d

3 Read and write. (6 points)

Would   like   grey   I'd   Yes   wouldn't

Would you ¹_____ a shirt?

²_____, I would.

³_____ like a blue shirt.

⁴_____ you like a yellow jumper?

No, I ⁵_____.

I'd like a ⁶_____ jumper.

4 Draw what you are wearing and write. (6 points)

These are my clothes.

I'm wearing _____.

_____

_____

_____

Score: ____ /25

1 Listen and number. (4 points)

a   b   c   d

2 Listen and ✓ or ✗. (5 points)

a   b   c   d   e

3 Draw a nurse and a firefighter. Then say. (6 points)

I'm a ...

I'm wearing ...

I'm not wearing ...

Score: ___ /15

Whole test score: ___ /40

1 Write. (5 points)

1 (green) (shoes.) (wearing) (I'm) _____

2 (a) (dress.) (I'm) (not) (wearing) (yellow) _____

3 (a) (white) (Are) (wearing) (jacket?) (you) _____

4 (you) (What) (wearing?) (are) _____

5 (hat.) (I'm) (an) (orange) (wearing) _____

2 Read and write the letter. Then colour. (8 points)

1 I'm wearing green glasses. ☐

2 I'm wearing a black cap. ☐

3 I'm wearing yellow jeans. ☐

4 I'm wearing a purple coat. ☐

a

b

c

d

3 Read and write. (6 points)

(wouldn't   would   you   blue   like   I'd)

Would [1]_____ like a red shirt?

No, I [2]_____ .

[3]_____ like a red skirt.

Would you [4]_____ a coat?

Yes, I [5]_____ .

I'd like a [6]_____ coat.

4 Draw your favourite clothes and write. (6 points)

These are my favourite clothes.

I'm wearing _____ .

_____

_____

_____

Score: ____ /25

1 Listen and number. (4 points)

a b c d

2 Listen and ✓ or ✗. (5 points)

a b c d e

3 Draw a police officer and a chef. Then say. (6 points)

I'm a ...

I'm wearing ...

I'm not wearing ...

Score: ____ /15

Whole test score: ____ /40

1 **Read and match. (5 points)**

1 It's snowy.

2 It's windy.

3 It's stormy.

4 It's cloudy.

5 It's rainy.

2 **Look, match and write. (10 points)**

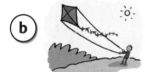

1 ride a _____

2 take a _____

3 go for a _____

4 make a _____

5 fly a _____

3 **Write. (4 points)**

1 weather | like? | the | What's _____

2 rainy | It's | today. _____

3 like | days. | I | rainy | don't _____

4 days. | I | sunny | like _____

4 **Draw the weather today and write. (6 points)**

This is the weather today.

It's _____ today.

It isn't _____.

I'm wearing _____.

I like/don't like _____.

Score: ____ /25

© Pearson Education Limited 2017   PHOTOCOPIABLE

  Listen and number. (4 points)

a  ☐

b  ☐

c ☐

d  ☐

  Listen and match. (5 points)

a

b

1 It's windy today.
2 It's sunny today.
3 It's snowy today.
4 It's cloudy today.
5 It's rainy today.

c

d

e

3 Ask and answer. (6 points)

What's the weather like today?

Do you like cloudy/ sunny/rainy days?

Which months are hot/cold in your country?

Do you like hot/cold/freezing/warm weather?

Score: ___ /15

Whole test score: ___ /40

1 **Read and match. (5 points)**

1 It's stormy.

2 It's cloudy.

3 It's windy.

4 It's rainy.

5 It's snowy.

2 **Look, match and write. (10 points)**

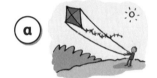

1 take a _____

2 fly a _____

3 make a _____

4 ride a _____

5 go for a _____

3 **Write. (4 points)**

1 (weather)(like)(What's)(the)(today?) _____

2 (cloudy)(It's)(today.) _____

3 (days.)(like)(windy)(I) _____

4 (don't)(cloudy)(I)(days.)(like) _____

4 **Draw your favourite weather and write. (6 points)**

This is my favourite weather.

It's _____.

I'm wearing _____.

I like _____ days.

I don't like _____ days.

Score: ____ /25

1 **Listen and number. (4 points)**

 a
 b
 c
 d

 2 **Listen and match. (5 points)**

 a

b

1 It's windy today.
2 It's sunny today.
3 It's snowy today.
4 It's cloudy today.
5 It's rainy today.

 c

 d

 e

3 **Ask and answer. (6 points)**

What's the weather like in your country?

Do you like cloudy/sunny/rainy days?

Do you ride a bike/read a book on sunny/rainy days?

What's your favourite weather?

Score: ___ /15

Whole test score: ___ /40

1 Read and match. (6 points)

1 What are these?
2 What's that?
3 Who's she?
4 Where's your daughter?
5 Who's he?
6 Can you do cartwheels?

a She's my aunt.
b It's a kite.
c He's my cousin.
d They're bikes.
e She's in the hall.
f Yes, I can.

2 Read and match. (4 points)

1 He's my uncle.

a

2 They're dolls.

b

3 She can swing.

c

4 She's in her bedroom.

d

Score: ___ /10

End of term 1

3 **Read. Then look and match. (4 points)**

 **a**  **b**  **c** 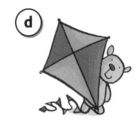 **d**

1 There are two teddy bears in the box.

3 There are two teddy bears under the chair.

2 There's a teddy bear behind the kite.

4 There's a teddy bear on the bed.

4 **Read and answer. (5 points)**

1 What day is it today? _____

2 When's your birthday? _____

3 Do you like Sundays? _____

4 Where's your cousin? _____

5 Can you stand on your head? _____

5 **Draw your bedroom and write. (6 points)**

This is my bedroom.

There's a _____.

There are _____.

They're _____.

Score: ___ /15

6 **Listen. Then match and write the numbers. (8 points)**

1 Sarah **2** Peter **3** Rick **4** Melisa

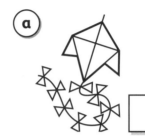 a

 b

 c

 d

7 **Listen and write. (6 points)**

JACK

1 Who?
_____

2 How old?
He's _____.

SUE

3 Who?
_____

4 Where? She's in the
_____.

JANE

5 Who?
_____

6 Birthday? It's in
_____.

8 **Draw toys and say. (6 points)**

bike   lorry   ball   helicopter   bus   motorbike

There are four cars.

They're in the kitchen, under the table.

Score: ____ /20

9 🎧 **Listen and ✓ or ✗. (8 points)**

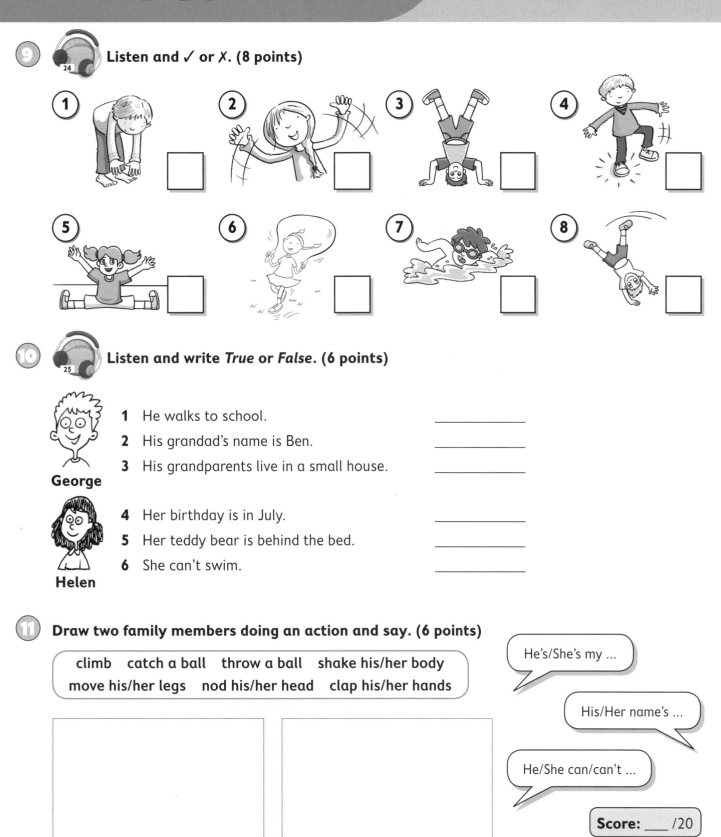

10 🎧 **Listen and write *True* or *False*. (6 points)**

George

1 He walks to school. _____

2 His grandad's name is Ben. _____

3 His grandparents live in a small house. _____

Helen

4 Her birthday is in July. _____

5 Her teddy bear is behind the bed. _____

6 She can't swim. _____

11 **Draw two family members doing an action and say. (6 points)**

climb   catch a ball   throw a ball   shake his/her body
move his/her legs   nod his/her head   clap his/her hands

He's/She's my …

His/Her name's …

He/She can/can't …

Score: ___ /20

Whole test score: ___ /65

1 **Read and match. (5 points)**

1 Have you got big eyes?

2 Is there any pasta?

3 What's that?

4 Is it a sheep?

5 Do you like coconut?

a Yes, it is.

b No, I don't.

c Yes, I have.

d No, there isn't.

e It's a skunk.

2 **Read and draw. (6 points)**

1 He's got big eyes, a small nose and a big mouth.

2 She's got short, curly hair and big eyes. She's got a small mouth.

3 **Look, read and write. (4 points)**

   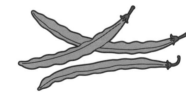

1 What's that?
It's a _____.

2 Is it a bat?
No, it's an
_____.

3 Is there any rice?
_____

4 Are there any beans?
_____

Score: ___ /15

4 **Read and answer. (4 points)**

1 Are there any bats in your attic? _____

2 Is there a lizard in your garden? _____

3 Has your mum got long hair? _____

4 Do you like pancakes? _____

5 **Read and write the letter. (4 points)**

1 He's got curly hair. ☐

2 Her hair is long and dark. ☐

3 She's got blond hair. ☐

4 He's got messy hair. ☐

a  b  c  d

6 **Look and write. (3 points)**

1 _____ 2 _____ 3 _____

7 **Look and write. Use *some* and *any*. (4 points)**

There's ...   There are ...   There isn't ...   There aren't ...

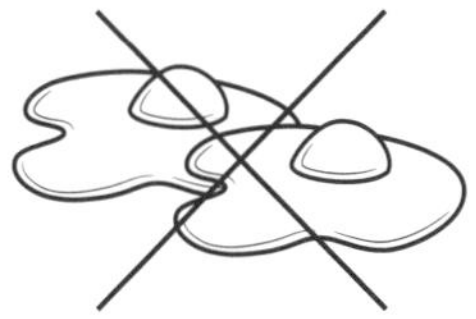

1 _____
_____

2 _____
_____

3 _____
_____

4 _____
_____

Score: ____ /15

8 **Listen and circle. (8 points)**

Tim

1 Tim's got a (small / big) face.

2 He's got big (ears / eyes).

3 He's got a pink (mouth / nose).

4 He's got (blond / brown) hair.

Claire

5 Claire's got a (small / big) nose.

6 She's got (small / big) ears.

7 She hasn't got a big (mouth / nose).

8 She's got (black / brown) hair.

  9 **Listen and ✓. (6 points)**

1 a  b    2 a  b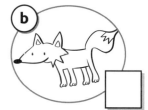

3 a  b    4 a 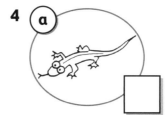 b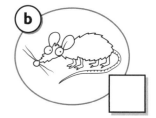

5 a  b    6 a  b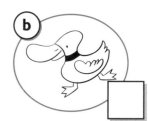

10 **Draw a family member's face and say. (6 points)**

mum   dad   aunt   uncle   granny   grandad   cousin

This is my ...

He's/She's got ...

He/She hasn't got ...

His/Her ... is ...

Score: ___ /20

11 🎧 28 **Listen and ✓ or ✗. (8 points)**

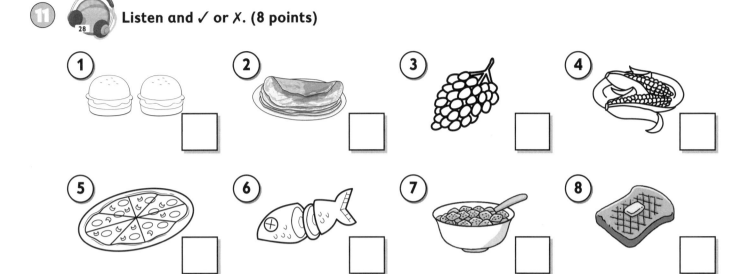

12 🎧 29 **Listen and write. (6 points)**

	Favourite animal	Favourite food for breakfast	Favourite food for lunch
Katie	1 _____	2 _____	3 _____
Charles	4 _____	5 _____	6 _____

13 **Draw three animals and three foods in the picture. Then ask and answer. (6 points)**

Is there a/any ...?

Yes, there is/are. It's/They're ...

Are there any ...?

No, there isn't/aren't.

Score: ____ /20

Whole test score: ____ /70

1 **Read and match. (6 points)**

1 What would you like?

2 Are you wearing a white shirt?

3 What's your favourite weather?

4 Would you like a yellow jacket?

5 What's the weather like today?

6 Do you like rainy days?

a Yes, I am.

b It's sunny.

c I'd like a red jumper.

d No, I don't.

e I like cloudy days.

f Yes, I would.

2 **Look and write. (8 points)**

1

2

3

4

_____

_____

_____

_____

5

6

7

8

_____

_____

_____

_____

3 **Read and answer. (6 points)**

1 What day is it today? _____

2 Are you wearing a white shirt? _____

3 Would you like yellow and red socks? _____

4 What would you like? _____

5 What's the weather like in December? _____

6 Do you like snowy days? _____

Score: ___ /20

4 **Look and write. (5 points)**

1 It's _____.   2 It's _____.   3 It's _____.   4 It's _____.   5 It's _____.

5 **Look and write. (3 points)**

1 Monday   2 Tuesday   3 Wednesday   4 Thursday

1 It's _Monday_. _Let's ride a bike_ _____.

2 It's Tuesday. Let's _____.

3 It's _____.

4 _____.

6 **Draw the weather and activities. Then write. (7 points)**

On _sunny_ days,

I _____.

On _____ days,

I _____.

On _____,

I _____.

On _____

_____.

Score: ___ /15

7 **Listen and number. (5 points)**

a    **b**    **c**    **d**    **e**

☐   ☐   ☐   ☐   ☐

8 **Listen and write. (4 points)**

1 I'm wearing a _____.

2 I'd like some _____.

3 Jack's _____ are blue.

4 I'm not wearing _____.

9 **Look and say. (6 points)**

I'm a ...   I'm wearing ...   I'm not wearing ...

Score: ___ /15

10 **Listen and match. (4 points)**

Monday	Tuesday	Wednesday	Thursday

11 **Listen and number. (5 points)**

12 **Look and say. (6 points)**

 It's ...

 Let's ...

 I like ... days.

 I don't like ... days.

Score: ___ /15

Whole test score: ___ /65

1 **Read and write *True* or *False*. (5 points)**

> I'm Ron. This is my house. This is my bedroom. It's small. There's a bed. My teddy bear is on the bed. My toy trains and cars are under the bed. The living room is big. My aunt and uncle are in the living room. My cousin is called Simon. He's got short, brown hair. It's curly. He's next to my aunt on the sofa. My uncle is on a big chair. Mum and Dad are in the kitchen.

1 Ron's bedroom is small. _____

2 There's a teddy bear under the bed. _____

3 There's a big living room. _____

4 Ron's cousin has got short hair. _____

5 Ron's uncle is on the sofa. _____

2 **Read and choose. (5 points)**

> I'm Harry. There's a small farm next to my house. There are lots of animals. My favourite animal is a sheep. It's white and it's got four legs. There are eight goats and five cows. The goats are white and the cows are brown. There are some hens and ducks. There aren't any horses. Today's cold and rainy. The cows and sheep are under the trees. I'm in my bedroom. I don't like cold and rainy days.

1 There's a farm
  a behind Harry's house.
  b next to Harry's house.
  c under Harry's house.

3 There aren't any
  a hens.
  b ducks.
  c horses.

5 Harry is
  a in the kitchen.
  b in his bedroom.
  c in the farm.

2 The sheep is Harry's
  a friend.
  b favourite book.
  c favourite animal.

4 The weather isn't
  a rainy.
  b sunny.
  c cold.

Score: _____ /10

1 Read and answer. (6 points)

1 Can you ride a bike? _____
2 Do you like rainy days? _____
3 Are you wearing black shoes? _____
4 Have you got blue eyes? _____
5 Can your friend swim? _____
6 How many cousins have you got? _____

2 Write. (4 points)

1 (bikes) (there?) (How many) (are) _____
2 (swim?) (you) (Can) _____
3 (your) (Are) (eyes) (big?) _____
4 (got) (curly) (Have) (hair?) (you) _____

3 Look and answer. (3 points)

1 What would you like?

_____

2 Is it a frog?

_____

3 What's the weather like?

_____

4 Draw a sunny day and write. (6 points)

Do you like sunny days?

_____

What are you wearing?

_____

What's your favourite weather?

_____

Score: ____ /19

  Listen. Then draw and colour. (6 points)

  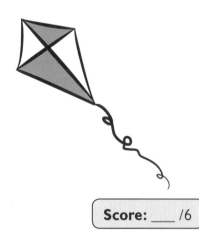

Score: ____ /6

 PHOTOCOPIABLE

1 **Find five differences. (10 points)**

Picture A

Picture B

In my picture there is/are …

Is there a/an …?

I can/can't see …

Is the … in/ on/under the …?

The … is in/ on/under/ next to the …

Where's the …?

Score: ____ /10

Whole test score: ____ /45

1 Read and write *True* or *False*. (5 points)

> I'm Ian and I'm eight. I like weekends and I like windy days. Today is Sunday and it's sunny and windy. Look! This is my kite. It's green and blue. It's big. This is my garden. I'm in the garden. It's big. I can fly my kite in the garden. Sally's my sister. She's in the garden. She's got a small kite. It's a red and purple kite. Toby is in the garden. Toby is my dog. He likes windy days.

1 It's rainy today.   _____

2 Ian's kite is green and blue.   _____

3 Ian can't fly his kite in the garden.   _____

4 Ian's sister is in the house.   _____

5 Ian's dog likes windy days.   _____

2 Read and choose. (5 points)

> Hi, I'm Nicola. It's Monday. I'm at school. It's lunch. I've got my lunchbox. I haven't got a banana or an apple. I've got some chicken and water. My friend Sue has got a burger and some grapes. Today it's rainy. I like rainy days. I can read my book in the classroom. My friend doesn't like rainy days. She likes sunny days. Today she can't run in the playground.

1 It's
  a windy.
  b Monday.
  c hot.

3 Nicola hasn't got any
  a fruit.
  b water.
  c chicken.

5 Sue doesn't like
  a pasta.
  b Mondays.
  c rainy days.

2 Nicola is
  a in the playground.
  b at school.
  c in the shop.

4 Sue is
  a Nicola's friend.
  b wearing trainers.
  c eight.

Score: ___ /10

1 Read and answer. (6 points)

1 Can you climb trees? _____
2 When's your birthday? _____
3 How many aunts have you got? _____
4 Do you like toast for breakfast? _____
5 Can your friend do cartwheels? _____
6 Have you got a big nose? _____

2 Write. (4 points)

1 (you?) (How) (are) _____

2 (are) (wearing?) (What) (you) _____

3 (cousins) (you) (have) (How many) (got?) _____

4 (short) (got) (hair?) (Have) (you) _____

3 Look and answer. (3 points)

1 What would you like?

_____

2 Has she got long hair?

_____

3 Is it a crow?

_____

4 Draw a rainy day and write. (6 points)

Do you like rainy days?

_____

What are you wearing?

_____

What's your favourite weather?

_____

Score: ____ /19

1   **Listen. Then draw and colour. (6 points)**

 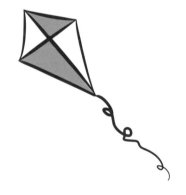 

Score: ____ /6

1 Find five differences. (10 points)

Picture A

Picture B

In my picture there is/are …

Is there a/an …?

I can/can't see …

Is the … in/on/under the …?

The … is in/on/under/next to the …

Where's the …?

Score: ___ /10

Whole test score: ___ /45

1 **Look and read. Then ✓ or ✗. (4 points)**

①  This is a boat. ☐

②  This is a sheep. ☐

③  These are trousers. ☐

④ These are beans. ☐

2 **Look and read. Then write *Yes* or *No*. (5 points)**

1 There's a ball under the bed. _____

2 The girl's got three teddy bears. _____

3 Her mum's got a book. _____

4 The dog's on the bed. _____

5 Her mum's hair is dark. _____

Score: ___ /9

     PHOTOCOPIABLE

3 **Look. Then find and write. (4 points)**

1  _____ iydwn

2 _____ sparge

3 _____ kskusn

4 **12** _____ veltwe

4 **Read and write. (5 points)**

arms   cold   coat   orange   hot

I'm under a ¹_____. I'm ²_____.

You wear me when it's ³_____, not when it's ⁴_____.

I've got two ⁵_____. What am I? I'm a jumper.

Score: ____ /9

Exam preparation

1   **Listen and match. (5 points)**

Anna

Sam

Olly

Tammy

George

2   **Listen and write. (5 points)**

1 Name of film: _____

2 Go with Mandy and _____

3 Cinema is in _____ Road.

4 Go to cinema by _____

5 Time film starts at _____ o'clock.

Score: ____ /10

3 **Listen and ✓. (2 points)**

1 What's in Sally's lunchbox?

(a)

(b)

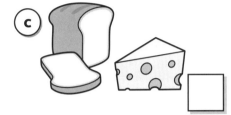

(c)

2 What's the weather like today?

(a)

(b)

(c)

4 **Listen and colour. (5 points)**

Score: ____ /7

1 Look and read. Then write ✓ or X. (4 points)

1  It's a skirt. ☐

2  His hair is long. ☐

3  It's sunny today. ☐

4  These are pancakes. ☐

2 Look and read. Then write *Yes* or *No*. (5 points)

1 There's a cat next to the girl. _____

2 The girl hasn't got boots. _____

3 The snowman hasn't got a hat. _____

4 The snowman's got a big nose. _____

5 It's snowy. _____

Score: ___ /9

3 **Look. Then find and write. (4 points)**

1

_____ wtyten

2

_____ drizal

3

_____ irenstar

4

_____ bnase

4 **Read and write. (5 points)**

| night   teddy bear   bed   pyjamas   house |

I'm in a ¹_____. There's a ²_____.

I'm wearing my ³_____ and I've got my ⁴_____.

I sleep here at ⁵_____. Where am I? I'm in my bedroom.

Score: ____ /9

Listen and match. (5 points)

George

Anna

Tammy

Sam

Olly

  Listen and write. (5 points)

1 Name of film: _____

2 Go with Mandy and _____

3 Cinema is in _____ Road.

4 Go to cinema by _____

5 Time film starts at _____ o'clock.

Score: ____ /10

3 **Listen and ✓. (2 points)**

1 What's in Sally's lunch box?

a

b

c

2 What's the weather like today?

a

b

c

 4 **Listen and colour. (5 points)**

Score: ___ /7

1 **Look and say. What's in the pictures? (8 points)**

There is/isn't …

There are/aren't …

He's got …

Score: ___ /8

2 Find five differences. (10 points)

Picture A

Picture B

Score: ___ /10

3 **Look and say. What's in the pictures? (8 points)**

snowy/windy/sunny/rainy   like/don't like

1

It's Monday. It's …

2

It's Tuesday …

3

It's …

4

It's …

Score: ___ /8

4 **Look and say. What's in the living room? (6 points)**

5 **Look and tell your partner to do the actions. (8 points)**

Score: ___ /14

Whole test score: ___ /75

Answer Key

Placement

Reading

1 1 this, c 2 's, f 3 your, e 4 Has, a 5 Is, d 6 Do, b

2 1 c 2 d 3 f 4 b 5 e 6 a (and colouring)

3 1 thirty, 30 2 twenty-seven, 27 3 fifty, 50
4 forty-three, 43 5 thirty-nine, 39 6 twenty, 20

Writing

1 1 's 2 are 3 Have 4 haven't 5 would 6 's

2 (open answers)

3 (open answers)

Listening and speaking

1 1 10 yellow bikes 2 15 blue cars 3 12 green kites
4 19 brown boats 5 14 purple trains

2 five, house, uncle, dog, garden, twelve, green, bike

3 1 eleven 2 boat 3 yellow 4 kite 5 kitchen 6 point

4 (example answers) It's a (goat/sheep/cow). It's got (four legs/a long tail/a short tail).

Unit 1

Reading and writing A

1 1 these, b 2 that, c 3 colour, d 4 bikes, a

2 1 f 2 b 3 e 4 a 5 c 6 d (and colouring)

3 1 toys 2 twenty 3 these 4 motorbike

4 (open answers)

Listening and speaking A

1 1 True 2 False 3 False 4 True 5 True

2 1 b, 1 2 a, 25 3 d, 13 4 c, 27

3 a 3 (red) b 1 (blue and green) c 4 (green) d 2 (red and yellow)

4 (example answers) There are (three bikes). It's a (teddy bear). They're (dolls).

Reading and writing B

1 1 that, c 2 those, a 3 colour, d 4 kites, b

2 1 a 2 c 3 f 4 d 5 b 6 e (and colouring)

3 1 fifty 2 those 3 bikes 4 lorry

4 (open answers)

Listening and speaking B

1 1 False 2 True 3 True 4 False 5 False

2 1 b, 1 2 c, 25 3 a, 13 4 d, 27

3 a 4 (green) b 1 (blue and green) c 2 (red and yellow)
d 3 (red)

4 (example answers) There are (six trains). It's a (ball). They're (boats).

Unit 2

Reading and writing A

1 1 c 2 a 3 d 4 b

2 1 b 2 a 3 d 4 e 5 c

3 1 house 2 bedrooms 3 kitchen 4 cousin 5 parents

4 (open answers)

Listening and speaking A

1 1 2 uncles 2 3 aunts 3 6 cousins 4 1 brother

2 aunt: living room uncle: attic granny: bedroom
cousin: kitchen grandad: living room

3 (example answers) There are (two bedrooms). The (kitchen) is next to the (bathroom).

Reading and writing B

1 1 b 2 d 3 a 4 c

2 1 c 2 e 3 a 4 b 5 d

3 1 flat 2 bathrooms 3 grandparents 4 living room
5 aunt

4 (open answers)

Listening and speaking B

1 1 6 uncles 2 8 aunts 3 17 cousins 4 1 sister

2 aunt: living room uncle: attic granny: bedroom
cousin: kitchen grandad: living room

3 (example answers) He's/She's my (grandad/granny). They're my (brothers).

Unit 3

Reading and writing A

1 1 c 2 b 3 a 4 d

2 1 d 2 b 3 a 4 c

3 1 Can you climb? 2 Can you swim?
3 Can you catch a ball? 4 Can you do cartwheels?

4 (open answers)

Listening and speaking A

1 a 3 b 4 c 1 d 2 e 5 f 6

2 Bob: can swim, stand on his head; can't climb, do the splits
Mel: can climb, swim, do the splits, stand on her head

3 (example answers) Can you (swim)? Yes, I can. /
No, I can't. I can/can't (stand on my head).

Reading and writing B

1 1 b 2 d 3 c 4 a

2 1 c 2 b 3 d 4 a

3 1 Can you do the splits? 2 Can you skip?
3 Can you touch your toes? 4 Can you swing?

4 (open answers)

Listening and speaking B

1 a 1 b 5 c 4 d 6 e 3 f 2

2 Mel: can climb, swim, do the splits, stand on her head
Bob: can swim, stand on his head; can't climb, do the splits

3 (example answers) Can you (touch your toes)?
Yes, I can. / No, I can't. I can/can't (wave my arms).

Unit 4
Reading and writing A
1 1 b   2 d   3 c   4 a

2 1 b   2 a   3 e   4 f   5 d   6 c

3 1 Have you got small ears?
2 Have you got short, dark hair?
3 Have you got brown eyes?
4 Have you got long, straight hair?

4 (open answers)

Listening and speaking A
1 1 True   2 True   3 False   4 False   5 True   6 False
7 True   8 False

2 Dorothy: long, straight, messy
Mick: short, curly, neat

3 (example questions and answers) Has he/she got
(a small nose)? Yes, he/she has. / No, he/she hasn't.
He's/She's got (long hair). He/She hasn't got (big ears).

Reading and writing B
1 1 c   2 a   3 b   4 d

2 1 d   2 b   3 c   4 a   5 f   6 e

3 1 Have you got long, straight hair?
2 Have you got blue eyes?
3 Have you got messy hair?
4 Have you got short, curly hair?

4 (open answers)

Listening and speaking B
1 1 False   2 False   3 True   4 True   5 False   6 True
7 False   8 True

2 Dorothy: long, straight, messy
Mick: short, curly, neat

3 (example questions and answers) Have you got (a small
nose)? Yes, I have. / No, I haven't. I've got (long hair).
I haven't got (big ears).

Unit 5
Reading and writing A
1 1 c   2 b   3 a

2 1 b   2 e   3 f   4 c   5 a   6 d

3 1 Are the hens big?   2 Are the goats white?   3 Are the
ducks long?   4 Are the bats black?   5 Are they foxes?

4 (open answers)

Listening and speaking A
1 a 4   b 1   c 5   d 2   e 3

2 c, e, f, g

3 (example questions and answers) Is it (a horse)? Yes, it
is. / No, it isn't. It's got/hasn't got (big eyes). Are they
(big/long/fast)? Yes, they are. / No, they aren't.

Reading and writing B
1 1 a   2 c   3 b

2 1 e   2 d   3 c   4 a   5 f   6 b

3 1 Are the hens small?   2 Are the bats white?
3 Are the lizards short?   4 Are they foxes?
5 Are the goats white?

4 (open answers)

Listening and speaking B
1 a 5   b 2   c 4   d 1   e 3

2 a, c, d, h

3 (example questions and answers) Is it (a horse)? Yes, it
is. / No, it isn't. It's got/hasn't got (big eyes). Are they
(big/long/fast)? Yes, they are. / No, they aren't.

Unit 6
Reading and writing A
1 1 apples   2 toast   3 eggs   4 pizza (and pictures)

2 1 I don't like coconut.   2 I like grapes.   3 I like pasta.
4 I don't like pineapple.

3 1 Is there any pasta?   2 Are there any beans?
3 There are some bananas.   4 Do you like sweetcorn?
5 Does Harry like toast?

4 (open answers)

Listening and speaking A
1 1 pizza, cheese, cereal, bananas
2 bread, toast, rice, chicken

2 Sally likes pineapple, cereal and toast. She doesn't like
sweetcorn, pancakes or coconut.

3 (example questions and answers) Is there any (milk)?
Are there any (bananas)? (Yes, there is/are. / No, there
isn't/aren't.) There's some (salad). There are some
(grapes). There isn't any (pizza). There aren't any
(apples).

Reading and writing B
1 1 chicken   2 salad   3 rice   4 burgers (and pictures)

2 1 I like pasta.   2 I like beans.   3 I don't like toast.
4 I don't like potatoes.

3 1 Is there any salad?   2 Are there any grapes?
3 Does Helen like cereal?   4 Do you like fish?
5 There are some apples.

4 (open answers)

Listening and speaking B
1 1 pizza, cheese, cereal, bananas
2 bread, toast, rice, chicken

2 Laurence likes pancakes, coconut and toast. He doesn't
like sweetcorn, pineapple or cereal.

3 (example questions and answers) Is there any (milk)? Are
there any (bananas)? (Yes, there is/are. / No, there isn't/
aren't.) There's some (salad). There are some (grapes).
There isn't any (pizza). There aren't any (apples).

Unit 7

Reading and writing A

1 1 I'm wearing trousers.   2 I'm not wearing a T-shirt.
3 Are you wearing a hat?   4 What are you wearing?
5 I'm wearing a pink skirt.

2 1 c   2 a   3 b   4 d (and colouring)

3 1 like   2 Yes   3 I'd   4 Would   5 wouldn't   6 grey

4 (open answers)

Listening and speaking A

1 a 3   b 4   c 1   d 2

2 a ✓   b ✗   c ✗   d ✓   e ✓

3 (example answers) I'm a nurse/firefighter. I'm wearing
(a hat/white trousers). I'm not wearing (a coat).

Reading and writing B

1 1 I'm wearing green shoes.   2 I'm not wearing a yellow
dress.   3 Are you wearing a white jacket?
4 What are you wearing?   5 I'm wearing an orange hat.

2 1 c   2 a   3 b   4 d (and colouring)

3 1 you   2 wouldn't   3 I'd   4 like   5 would   6 blue

4 (open answers)

Listening and speaking B

1 a 4   b 1   c 2   d 3

2 a ✓   b ✓   c ✓   d ✗   e ✗

3 (example answers) I'm a police officer/chef. I'm wearing
(a blue hat/a white shirt). I'm not wearing (a helmet).

Unit 8

Reading and writing A

1 1 c   2 a   3 e   4 d   5 b

2 1 bike, a   2 photo, e   3 walk, d   4 snowman, c
5 kite, b

3 1 What's the weather like?   2 It's rainy today.
3 I don't like rainy days.   4 I like sunny days.

4 (open answers)

Listening and speaking A

1 a 3   b 2   c 1   d 4

2 1 b   2 a   3 d   4 c   5 e

3 (example answers) It's (cold) today. I like (sunny) days.
(July/August) is (hot) in my country. I like (warm)
weather.

Reading and writing B

1 1 e   2 d   3 a   4 b   5 c

2 1 photo, c   2 kite, a   3 snowman, e   4 bike, d
5 walk, b

3 1 What's the weather like today?   2 It's cloudy today.
3 I like windy days.   4 I don't like cloudy days.

4 (open answers)

Listening and speaking B

1 a 2   b 4   c 3   d 1

2 1 e   2 c   3 a   4 b   5 d

3 (example answers) We have (hot and cold) weather in
my country. I like (rainy) days. I (read a book) on (rainy)
days. My favourite weather is (sunny) weather.

End of term 1

Reading and writing

1 1 d   2 b   3 a   4 e   5 c   6 f

2 1 c   2 a   3 d   4 b

3 1 b   2 d   3 c   4 a

4 (open answers)

5 (open answers)

Listening and speaking

6 1 b, 25   2 d, 30   3 a, 14   4 c, 50

7 1 uncle   2 33   3 granny   4 kitchen   5 cousin
6 February

8 (example answers) There's a bike in the kitchen.
There are two buses. They're under the bed.

9 1 ✓   2 ✓   3 ✗   4 ✓   5 ✓   6 ✗   7 ✗   8 ✓

10 1 True   2 False   3 True   4 False   5 False   6 True

11 (example answers) He's my (grandad). His name's (John).
He can't (climb). He can (nod his head).

End of term 2

Reading and writing

1 1 c   2 d   3 e   4 a   5 b

2 (pictures)

3 1 duck   2 owl   3 No, there isn't.   4 Yes, there are.

4 (open answers)

5 1 d   2 c   3 b   4 a

6 1 horse   2 hen   3 frog

7 1 There aren't any eggs.   2 There's some salad.
3 There isn't any chicken.   4 There are some bananas.

Listening and speaking

8 1 big   2 eyes   3 nose   4 blond   5 small   6 big
7 mouth   8 black

9 1 b   2 b   3 a   4 b   5 a   6 a

10 (example answers) This is my (mum). She's got (curly
hair). She hasn't got (a big nose). Her (eyes) are (blue).

11 1 ✗   2 ✓   3 ✓   4 ✓   5 ✗   6 ✗   7 ✓   8 ✗

12 1 sheep   2 eggs   3 pasta   4 frog   5 pancakes   6 salad

13 (example questions and answers) Is there (a banana)?
Yes, there is. It's (on the table). Are there any (frogs)?
No, there aren't.

End of term 3

Reading and writing

1 1 c   2 a   3 e   4 f   5 b   6 d

2 1 shoes   2 dress   3 trousers   4 socks   5 T-shirt
6 coat   7 hat   8 jumper

3 (open answers)

4 1 windy   2 cloudy   3 snowy   4 sunny   5 rainy

5 **1** It's Monday. Let's ride a bike.   **2** It's Tuesday. Let's make a snowman.   **3** It's Wednesday. Let's go for a walk.   **4** It's Thursday. Let's fly a kite.

6 (open answers)

Listening and speaking

7 **a** 5   **b** 2   **c** 1   **d** 4   **e** 3

8 **1** coat   **2** jeans   **3** glasses   **4** boots

9 (example answers) I'm a (firefighter). I'm wearing (a helmet). I'm not wearing (a dress).

10 Monday, c   Tuesday, d   Wednesday, a   Thursday, b

11 **a** 4   **b** 1   **c** 5   **d** 2   **e** 3

12 (example answers) It's (windy). I like/don't like (snowy) days. On (rainy) days, I wear (boots).

Final

Reading A

1 **1** True   **2** False   **3** True   **4** True   **5** False

2 **1** b   **2** c   **3** c   **4** b   **5** b

Writing A

1 (open answers)

2 **1** How many bikes are there?   **2** Can you swim?
3 Are your eyes big?   **4** Have you got curly hair?

3 **1** I'd like a jumper, please.   **2** No, it isn't. (It's a fox.)
3 It's windy.

4 (open answers)

Listening A and B

1 **1** a grey and blue doll on the bed   **2** a brown shoe under the bed   **3** a small red and green kite next to the bed

Speaking A

Differences: 1 A = It's a cloudy day. B = It's a sunny day.
2 A = There isn't a teddy bear on the bed. B = There's a/one teddy bear on the bed.   3 A = There's one book on the table next to the bed. B = There are two books on table next to the bed.   4 A = There aren't any toy cars under the bed. B = There are two toy cars under the bed.   5 A = The boy's hair is blond. B = The boy's hair is dark.

Reading B

1 **1** False   **2** True   **3** False   **4** False   **5** True

2 **1** b   **2** b   **3** a   **4** a   **5** c

Writing B

1 (open answers)

2 **1** How are you?   **2** What are you wearing?
3 How many cousins have you got?
4 Have you got short hair?

3 **1** I'd like a cap, please.   **2** Yes, she has.
3 No, it isn't. (It's an owl.)

4 (open answers)

Speaking B

Differences: **1** A = There's one coat. B = There are two coats.   **2** A = There's a/one sock on the floor next to Emily. B = There's a/one sock on the floor under the chair.   **3** A = There's a/one shoe next to the chair. B = There are two shoes

next to the chair.   **4** A = Her hair is dark. B = Her hair is blond.   **5** A = There's a pair of trousers on the chair. B = There aren't any trousers on the chair.

Exam preparation

Reading and writing A

1 **1** ✓   **2** ✗   **3** ✓   **4** ✗

2 **1** No   **2** No   **3** Yes   **4** No   **5** Yes

3 **1** windy   **2** grapes   **3** skunks   **4** twelve

4 **1** coat   **2** orange   **3** cold   **4** hot   **5** arms

Listening A

1 Olly = boy sitting on the bench, clapping his hands
Sam = girl with short, blond hair   George = boy with the ball   Anna = girl next to George (wearing shorts and a white T-shirt)   Tammy = girl next to Anna

2 **1** Night Animals   **2** Sue   **3** Park   **4** car   **5** 4/four

3 **1** c   **2** a

4 bird under the tree = green   bird on the house = blue
bird on the car = red head and yellow body and tail
bird behind the house = purple and pink   bird in the tree = orange head and brown body

Reading and writing B

1 **1** ✓   **2** ✗   **3** ✗   **4** ✓

2 **1** Yes   **2** No   **3** No   **4** Yes   **5** Yes

3 **1** twenty   **2** lizard   **3** trainers   **4** beans

4 **1** house   **2** bed   **3** pyjamas   **4** teddy bear   **5** night

Listening B

1 Olly = boy sitting on the bench, clapping his hands
Sam = girl with short, blond hair   George = boy with the ball   Anna = girl next to George (wearing shorts and a white T-shirt)   Tammy = girl next to Anna

2 **1** Night Animals   **2** Sue   **3** Park   **4** car   **5** 4/four

3 **1** b   **2** c

4 bird under the tree = green   bird on the house = blue
bird on the car = red head and yellow body and tail   bird behind the house = purple and pink   bird in the tree = orange head and brown body

Speaking A and B

1 (example answers) There's a (cat on the bed). There's a (boy). He's wearing (pyjamas). It's (sunny).

2 Differences: 1 A = The girl's eating pizza. B = The girl's eating chicken.   2 A = She's wearing a dress. B = She's wearing a T-shirt and trousers.   3 A = It's cloudy. B = It's sunny.   4 A = She's got a doll. B = She's got a train.
5 A = The dog is big. B = The dog is small.

3 (example answers) **1** It's Monday. It's sunny. I like sunny days.   **2** It's Tuesday. It's rainy. I don't like rainy days.
3 It's (Wednesday), I fly a kite. It's windy.
4 It's (Thursday), it's snowy. I make a snowman.

4 (example answers) There's a (painting). It's (above the sofa). There's a (TV). It's (next to the sofa).

5 Stamp your feet. Wave your arms. Shake your body. Touch your toes.

Audioscript

Audio files are available on the Active Teach, or at pearsonelt.com/islands.

M: Man

W: Woman

Placement

Placement Test. Test Booklet.
Activity 1. Listen and match.

1

W: How many bikes have you got?

M: I've got ten yellow bikes.

2

W: How many cars have you got?

M: I've got fifteen blue cars.

3

W: How many kites have you got?

M: I've got twelve. They're green.

4

W: Have you got any boats?

M: Yes, I have. I've got nineteen boats. They're brown.

5

W: And what about trains – how many trains have you got?

M: I've got fourteen purple trains.

Placement Test. Test Booklet.
Activity 2. Listen and ✓.

Hi. My name's Bob. I'm five. I live in a house next to the beach. In the house there are five people - my mum, my dad, my brother, my sister and me. My uncle has got a house in the town centre. I like my uncle. He's got a big furry dog called Bramble. At the weekend I play with Bramble in my uncle's garden. He's got a big garden. There are flowers and trees. The trees are apple trees. There are twelve apple trees! I ride my new green and red bike to my uncle's house.

Placement Test. Test Booklet.
Activity 3. Listen and write the missing letters.

1

M: How do you spell eleven?

W: Eleven? That's E-L-E-V-E-N.

2

M: How do you spell boat?

W: Boat ... That's B-O-A-T.

3

M: OK. And how do you write yellow?

W: That's easy. Y-E-L-L-O-W.

4

M: What about kite. How do you spell kite?

W: Umm. That's K-I-T-E.

5

M: OK. What about kitchen? How do you write kitchen?

W: K-I-T-C-H-E-N.

6

M: OK. Last one. How do you spell point?

W: Point? Point a finger?

M: Yes.

W: P-O-I-N-T.

M: They're all correct! Well done!

Unit 1

Unit 1 Tests A and B. Test Booklet.
Activity 1. Listen and write *True* or *False*.

1

W: Hi, Sam. When's your birthday?

M: My birthday's in October.

W: Is October your favourite month?

M: No. My favourite month is August.

2

M: Hi, Paula. What's your favourite month?

W: My favourite month is June. When's yours?

M: My favourite month is July. My birthday's in July.

W: My birthday's in June!

3

W: Hi, Jimmy. What's your favourite colour?

M: My favourite colour?

W: Yes. What's your favourite colour?

M: I've got two favourite colours.

W: Two? What are they?

M: Blue and white. My football team!

4

M: Hi, Sarah. What's your favourite day of the week?

W: My favourite day is Saturday. What's yours?

M: I like Saturday, too. But my favourite day is Sunday.

5

W: Hi, Barry. What's your favourite month?

M: My favourite month is October. I get some sweets at Halloween.

W: What is your favourite colour?

M: My favourite colour is brown. My dog is brown!

Unit 1 Tests A and B. Test Booklet.
Activity 2. Listen and match. Then write.

1

W: What's this, Charlie?

M: It's my birthday present.

W: What is it?

M: It's a boat.

2

M: Are these your presents, Sue?

W: Yes.

M: How many are there?

W: There are twenty-five!

M: Twenty-five presents?

3

W: How many toys are there in your bedroom, Harry?

M: Umm. There are thirteen.

W: Thirty toys?

M: No. THIRTEEN!

4

M: What are those, Helen?

W: Those are kites.

M: Kites?

W: Yes. They are kites.

M: How many kites are there?

W: Twenty-seven.

M: Twenty-seven kites?

W: Yes. I've got twenty seven friends at my birthday party.

Unit 1 Tests A and B. Test Booklet.
Activity 3. Listen and number. Then colour.

1

W: What's this?

M: It's a blue and green helicopter.

2

M: What are these?

W: They are red and yellow kites.

M: How many are there?

W: There are six!

3

M: How many buses are there?

W: There are seven buses.

M: Are they red?

W: Yes.

4

M: What are those?

W: They're planes.

M: Planes? How many are there?

W: There are four green planes.

Unit 2

Unit 2 Tests A and B. Test Booklet.
Activity 1. Listen and write the number.

1

M: Hi, Kim. Who's he?

W: He's my uncle.

M: How many uncles have you got?

W: I've got two uncles ... Uncle John and Uncle Harry.

M: I've got six uncles. Uncle Pete, Uncle Rob ...

W: OK! OK!

2

M: How many aunts have you got, Kim?

W: I've got three aunts. Aunt Susie, Aunt Rosie and Aunt Izzie. How many have you got, Andy?

M: I've got eight aunts. Aunt Patsy, Aunt Jo, Aunt Kate ...

W: OK! OK!

3

M: How many cousins have you got, Kim?

W: I've got six cousins. Gareth, Helen, Richard, Liam, Sandy and Charles. How many cousins have you got, Andy?

M: Well ... Umm ... there's three ... and two ... and four ... and one ... and three ... and two and two. How many is that?

W: That's sixteen!

M: Is it? Isn't it seventeen?

W: Ah yes. You're right. Wow. Seventeen cousins!

4

M: How many brothers and sisters have you got?

W: I've got one brother. And you?

M: I've got two brothers. And I've got one sister.

W: I've got two sisters, Zoe and Pam.

Unit 2 Tests A and B. Test Booklet.
Activity 2. Listen and match.

1

W: Where's my aunt?

M: She's in the living room.

2

W: Where's my uncle?

M: He's in the attic.

W: In the attic?

M: Yes. He's practising his violin!

3

W: Where's my granny?

M: Oh, she's in her bedroom.

4

W: Where's my cousin?

M: Angela? Cousin Angela's in the kitchen.

W: Is she hungry?

M: Yes. Look. She's got a cheese and tomato sandwich!

5

W: And ... where's grandad?

M: He's in the living room.

W: Oh yes. Look. He's on the sofa. He's got a book.

M: He's happy!

Unit 3

Unit 3 Tests A and B. Test Booklet.
Activity 1. Listen and number.

1

M: OK, everyone. Listen to me. Touch your toes.
OK? Touch your toes.

2

M: Clap your hands.
OK? Clap your hands.

3

M: Point your finger.
OK? Point your finger.

4

M: Stamp your feet.
OK? Stamp your feet.

5

M: Wave your arms.
OK? Wave your arms.

6

M: Shake your body.
OK? Shake your body.

Unit 3 Test A and B. Test Booklet.
Activity 2. Listen and ✓ or ✗.

1

W: Hi, Bob.

M: Hi, Mel.

W: Can you climb, Bob?

M: No, I can't. Can you?

W: Yes. Yes, I can climb. I can climb trees. I live in a tree-house!

2

W: Can you swim, Bob?

M: Yes, I can. I live on a house boat! Can you swim, Mel?

W: Yes. I can swim. I swim at school.

M: I swim at school, too!

3

W: Can you do the splits, Bob?

M: Ouch!!! No I can't! Can you?

W: Yes, I can. In dance class I do the splits.

M: Wow!

4

W: Can you stand on your head?

M: Yes, I can. I can stand on my head and count to ten! Can you?

W: Yes. I can stand on my head and count to two!

M: Hah!

Unit 4

Unit 4 Tests A and B. Test Booklet.
Activity 1. Listen and write *True* or *False*.

This is Gemma. She's got a small face. She's got a small, pink nose. She's got big eyes. They're blue. She's got brown hair. She hasn't got big ears. She's got a small mouth.
This is Brian. He's got big ears. He's got brown hair and brown eyes. He hasn't got a big mouth. He's got a big nose and a small face.

Unit 4 Tests A and B. Test Booklet.
Activity 2. Listen and ✓.

1

M: Dorothy is in my class.

W: Is her hair long?

M: Yes, it is.

W: Is her hair straight and neat?

M: Her hair is straight. It isn't neat. She's got messy hair!

W: She's got long, straight, messy hair?

M: Yes.

2

W: OK. And, Mick.

M: Mick's in your class. Is his hair short?

W: Yes, it is.

M: Is his hair straight?

W: No, it isn't. His hair isn't straight, it's curly.

M: Is it messy?

W: No, his hair isn't messy; it's neat.

M: He's got short, straight and neat hair?

W: No ... short, CURLY and neat hair!

Unit 5

Unit 5 Tests A and B. Test Booklet.
Activity 1. Listen and number.

1

M: What's this? It isn't big and it isn't very small. It's white. It's got four thin legs and a short white tail.

2

W: What's this? It's big and strong. It's got long hair on its head. It's got a long tail.

3

M: What's this? It's not very small. It's got wings and feathers.

4

W: What's this? It isn't big and it isn't small. It's got short white hair and a short tail. It isn't a sheep.

5

M: What's this? It's big. It's black and white. It's got four legs and a long tail. It hasn't got long hair on its head.

Unit 5 Tests A and B. Test Booklet.
Activity 2. Listen and ✓ the animals you hear.

W: In my garden there are animals. There are big animals and small animals, night animals and day animals.

M: What's that?

W: It's a frog. And that bird on the grass is a crow.

M: A frog and a crow. What's that bird in the tree? It's got big eyes.

W: That's an owl. That's a night animal.

M: Oh yes. Have you got a bat? Bats are my favourite animals.

W: Yes. I've got bats. At night there are bats in the garden. They fly in the garden. They are in the trees.

Unit 6
Unit 6 Tests A and B. Test Booklet.
Activity 1. Listen and ✓.
1

W: Hi Rich. Can I ask you some questions?

M: Yes, of course.

W: Look at the list. What's your favourite food?

M: Well ... I like pizza.

W: OK ... pizza.

M: I like cheese ...

W: ... and cheese ...

M: Yes, and I like cereal and bananas.

W: ... you like cereal and salad.

M: No ... cereal and bananas.

W: Sorry. Cereal and bananas.

2

W: OK. Now ... what food don't you like? Look at the list.

M: Well ... I don't like bread.

W: OK.

M: Umm. I like apples. Ah ... here! I don't like toast.

W: OK ... toast.

M: And ... Umm ... I don't like rice and chicken.

W: OK. Thank you.

Unit 6 Tests A and B. Test Booklet.
Activity 2. Listen and ✓ or ✗.
1

M: Does Sally like sweetcorn, Jenny?

W: No, she doesn't. She doesn't like sweetcorn. Does Laurence?

M: Laurence? No, Laurence doesn't like sweetcorn.

2

M: OK. What about pineapple. Does Sally like pineapple?

W: Yes, she does. She likes pineapple. And Laurence?

M: No, he doesn't. Laurence doesn't like pineapple.

3

M: OK. Does Sally like pancakes?

W: No, she doesn't. She doesn't like pancakes. Does Laurence?

M: Yes, he does. He likes pancakes.

4

M: What about cereal. Does Sally like cereal, Jenny?

W: Yes, she does. She likes cereal. And, what about Laurence, does he like cereal?

M: No, he doesn't like cereal.

5

M: Does Sally like coconut?

W: No, she doesn't. She doesn't like coconut. And Laurence, does he like coconut?

M: Laurence? Yes. Laurence likes coconut.

6

M: OK. Last question ... Does Sally like toast?

W: Toast? Yes, she does like toast. She likes toast for breakfast. And Laurence?

M: Yes. Laurence likes toast.

Unit 7
Unit 7 Tests A and B. Test Booklet.
Activity 1. Listen and number.
1

W: Hi, I'm Fiona. I'm wearing a dress and shoes. I'm not wearing socks.

2

M: Hi. I'm Paul. I'm wearing trousers and a T-shirt. I'm not wearing shoes. I'm wearing socks.

3

W: Hi. I'm Carrie, I'm wearing a skirt and a T-shirt. I'm not wearing shoes. I'm wearing big boots!

4

M: Hi, I'm Alfie. I'm not wearing a T-shirt or a jumper. I'm wearing my pyjamas!

Unit 7 Tests A and B. Test Booklet.
Activity 2. Listen and ✓ or ✗.
1

M: Hello. Can I help you?

W: Yes. I'd like a new dress. I'd like a purple dress.

M: Would you like a pair of trousers?

W: Yes, I would. I'd like a pair of brown trousers.

M: OK. Would you like a new pair of shoes?

W: No, I wouldn't. I'd like a pair of socks.

M: And would you like a T-shirt? There's a blue and white T-shirt and a red and yellow T-shirt.

W: No, thank you. I wouldn't.

M: OK. Thank you.

Unit 8
Unit 8 Tests A and B. Test Booklet.
Activity 1. Listen and number.

1

M: What's the weather like today?

W: It's snowy.

M: Let's make a snowman!

W: No, it's freezing!

2

W: It's warm today.

M: Let's go for a walk!

W: Great idea!

3

M: It's very hot today.

W: Let's go swimming!

4

W: Do you like cold weather?

W: Yes, I like cold weather. I read a book at home when it's cold.

Unit 8 Tests A and B. Test Booklet.
Activity 2. Listen and match.

1

W: It's windy today. Let's go and fly a kite.

M: Yes. That's a good idea.

2

W: It's sunny today. How about riding our bikes?

M: That's a great idea. My bike is in the garden next to yours.

3

W: It's snowy today. What do you want to do, Sam?

M: How about making a snowman?

W: OK. Let's make two snowmen.

4

W: It's cloudy today. Shall we stay in the house?

M: Yes. It's quite cold.

5

M: It's rainy today. What do you want to do, Carol?

W: How about reading a book?

M: Yes. That's a good idea.

End of term 1
End of term Test 1. Units 1–3. Test Booklet.
Activity 6. Listen. Then match and write the numbers.

1

M: What's your name?

W: I'm Sarah.

M: What are these? Are they boats?

W: Yes, they are.

M: How many boats are there?

W: Twenty-five!

2

W: Are these your trains, Peter?

M: Yes, they are.

W: How many trains are there?

M: There are thirty trains!

3

W: What are those, Rick?

M: They're my kites.

W: How many kites are there?

M: Erm ... one, two, ... five, six ... Fourteen.

W: Fourteen!

4

M: What toys are there in your bedroom, Melisa?

W: There are dolls.

M: How many dolls are there?

W: Fifty!

M: Fifteen?

W: No, fifty!

End of term Test 1. Units 1–3. Test Booklet.
Activity 7. Listen and write.

M: Hello. Who's he?

W: He's my uncle. His name's Jack.

M: How old is he?

W: He's thirty-three.

M: And who's she?

W: She's my granny. Her name's Sue.

M: Where is she now?

W: She's in the kitchen.

M: Is that your sister?

W: No, she's my cousin Jane. She's nine.

M: When is her birthday?

W: It's in February. My birthday is in January!

M: OK.

End of term Test 1. Units 1–3. Test Booklet.
Activity 9. Listen and ✓ or ✗.

1

W: Can you touch your toes?

M: Yes, I can!

2

M: Can you wave your arms?

W: Yes, I can!

3

W: Can you stand on your head?

M: No, I can't.

4

W: Can you stamp your feet?

M: Yes, I can.

5

M: Can you do the splits?

W: Yes, I can!

6

M: Can you skip?

W: No, I can't.

7

W: Can you swim?

M: No, I can't.

8

W: Can you do cartwheels?

M: Yes, I can.

End of term Test 1. Units 1–3. Test Booklet.
Activity 10. Listen and write *True* or *False*.

M: Hello. My name's George and I'm eight years old. My birthday is in August. I live in a flat and I walk to school with my mum or dad. I've got one uncle. His name's Ben. My grandad and my granny live in a small house. I go there every Sunday.

W: Hi! I'm Helen. I'm seven years old. My birthday is in December, but my favourite month is July. My favourite toy is my teddy bear. It's on my bed. I can swing and do cartwheels, but I can't swim.

End of term 2
End of term Test 2. Units 4–6. Test Booklet.
Activity 8. Listen and circle.

W: My friend's name is Tim. Tim's got a big happy face. He hasn't got big ears; he's got big eyes. He's got a pink nose and a red mouth. He's got long blond hair.

M: This is Claire. She's my cousin. Claire's got a small pink nose. She's got big ears. She hasn't got a big mouth; she's got a small mouth. She's got long black hair.

End of term Test 2. Units 4–6. Test Booklet.
Activity 9. Listen and ✓.

1

W: This animal is a bird. It's got wings. It can fly. It's black.

2

M: This animal isn't very big. It's got a long tail and big ears. It can't fly but it can run. It isn't black and white!

3

W: This animal is big. It's black and white. It's got a long tail. It's got big brown eyes.

4

M: This animal is small. It's got a long tail and big eyes. It's got four legs. It's got a nose and two ears.

5

W: This animal hasn't got wings. It's got small eyes and a small tail. It can't fly. It's got four legs.

6

W: This animal is big. It's white. It's got a black face and black legs.

End of term Test 2. Units 4–6. Test Booklet.
Activity 11. Listen and ✓ or ✗.

1

W: What's your favourite food? Do you like burgers?

M: No, I don't.

2

M: Do you like pancakes?

W: Mmmmm. Yes, I do!

M: Me too!

3

W: Does your sister like grapes?

M: Yes, she does. She likes all fruit.

4

M: Do you like sweetcorn for lunch?

W: Mmmm ... Yes, I do!

5

W: What about pizza?

M: Erm ... I don't like pizza.

6

M: Do you like fish?

W: Um ... No ... No, I don't like fish.

7

W: Does your cousin Alex like cereal?

M: Yes, he does. He likes it for breakfast.

8

M: And do you like toast for breakfast?

W: Erm ... No, I don't.

End of term Test 2. Units 4–6. Test Booklet.
Activity 12. Listen and write.

W: Have you got a sister?

M: Yes, I have. Her name's Katie.

W: What's your sister's favourite animal?

M: Her favourite animal is the sheep.

W: OK. And what's her favourite food?

M: She likes eggs for breakfast.

W: And what's her favourite food for lunch?

M: It's pasta.

W: OK, thank you.

M: Have you got a brother?

W: Yes, I have. His name's Charles.

M: What's Charles' favourite animal?

W: He likes owls and bats, but his favourite animal is the frog.

M: And what about food? What's his favourite breakfast?

W: His favourite breakfast is pancakes. He doesn't like cereal.

M: What about lunch? Does he like chicken?

W: No, he doesn't. His favourite food for lunch is salad.

M: Great! Thanks.

End of term 3

End of term Test 3. Units 7–8. Test Booklet.
Activity 7. Listen and number.

1

W: Hi I'm Pam. I'm wearing a dress and a hat.

2

M: Hi. I'm Paul. I'm wearing black and white pyjamas. They're my zebra pyjamas!

3

M: Hi, I'm Chris. I'm not wearing a T-shirt or pyjamas. I'm wearing my shoes, a jumper and a pair of trousers.

4

W: Hi. I'm Charlotte. I'm wearing a skirt, a T-shirt and white socks.

5

M: Hello. I'm Tom. I'm wearing trousers and shoes. I'm not wearing a jumper. I'm wearing a T-shirt.

End of term Test 3. Units 7–8. Test Booklet.
Activity 8. Listen and write.

1

W: My name's Tom. I'm not wearing a T-shirt. I'm wearing a coat because it's cold and snowy today!

2

W: Hello. What would you like?

M: I'd like some jeans, please.

W: OK. Would you like a jumper too?

M: No. No, thank you.

3

W: This is my cousin Jack. He's wearing a green cap and blue glasses.

4

M: Hi, I'm Chris. It isn't a rainy day. I'm not wearing boots. I'm wearing trainers because it's sunny and warm.

End of term Test 3. Units 7–8. Test Booklet.
Activity 10. Listen and match.

M: What's the weather like this week?

W: On Monday, it's sunny. That's good. Tuesday is a cloudy day ... Oh ... and it's windy on Wednesday. OK? You can fly your kite on Wednesday.

M: Great! What about Thursday?

W: On Thursday, it's snowy. And on Friday it's rainy.

M: OK. Thank you.

End of term Test 3. Units 7–8. Test Booklet.
Activity 11. Listen and number.

1

M: It's rainy today.

W: Let's watch TV.

M: No, let's read a book.

W: OK, sure.

2

W: Look. Do you like my snowman?

M: Yes! Well Done.

W: Let's take a photo.

M: OK. Say 'cheese'!

3

M: I'm bored. Let's go to the beach.

W: I'm tired.

M: OK. Let's watch TV then.

W: All right.

4

W: I like your bike.

M: Thanks. I like yours too.

W: Let's ride to the park.

M: Great idea!

5

M: I'm hot!

W: Yes, it's a very hot day. Let's go to the beach.

M: Yippie!

Final

Final Tests A and B. Test Booklet.
Activity 1. Listen. Then draw and colour.

1

W: Can you see the picture of the girl in bed?

M: Yes. Can I draw a doll on the bed?

W: Yes. Draw a doll on the bed.

M: What colour is the doll?

W: The doll's grey and blue.

M: There.

2

W: OK. Now I want you to draw a shoe under the bed.

M: A shoe? One shoe?

W: Yes. one shoe.

M: OK.

W: Colour the shoe brown.

M: OK. One brown shoe!

3

W: Can you draw a small kite next to the bed?

M: Yes. A small kite. Can I colour it red and green?

W: Yes, you can.

Exam preparation

Exam preparation Tests A and B. Test Booklet.
Activity 1. Listen and match.

1

M: Look at everybody. They're happy.

W: Yes. They're my friends.

M: Who's that over there?

W: Where?

M: Over there. He's clapping his hands.

W: That's Olly.

2

M: Who's that next to Olly? She looks happy.

W: The girl with the short, blond hair?

M: Is her name Sam?

W: Yes. Samantha. Sam is short for Samantha.

3

M: And ... can you see the boy with the ball?

W: The boy wearing white shorts?

M: Yes.

W: That's George. He likes ball games.

M: He can jump very high.

W: Yes, he can jump and catch and throw ... he doesn't like maths and history but he loves sport.

4

M: And who is the girl next to George?

W: The girl with the white shorts and grey T-shirt?

M: No. The girl with the white shorts and white T-shirt?

W: Oh yes. That's Anna. She's my best friend. She likes running and swimming. She can run fast.

5

M: OK. And one more. The girl next to Anna. What's her name?

W: That's Tammy. She's new.

M: Is she happy?

W: Yes. She is. She's very friendly and helpful.

M: What a nice friend.

W: Yes. Everybody likes her.

Exam preparation Tests A and B. Test Booklet.
Activity 2. Listen and write.

1

M: Can I go to the cinema this afternoon, mum?

W: Umm ... What film is on?

M: It's a new film. It's called 'Night Animals'.

W: Is it an under twelve film?

M: Yes. It's a children's cartoon film. It looks great.

2

W: OK. What about your friends Mandy and Sue. Do they want to go?

M: Yes. They want to see it. And they can go today.

W: OK.

M: So ... can I go?

3

W: Well ... Where is the film on?

M: It's on at the cinema in Park Road.

W: Oh, that's the one next to the sports centre.

M: Yes. That's it. So ... can I go?

4

W: OK. How are you going to get there?

M: Mandy's mum has got a car. She can take us there.

5

W: What time does it start?

M: The afternoon film starts at 4 o'clock.

Exam preparation Tests A and B. Test Booklet.
Activity 3. Listen and ✓.

1

M: What have you got for lunch today Sally?

W: I've got some bread.

M: Have you got pizza?

W: No ... I haven't got any pizza. I've got bread and ...

M: What's that?

W: That's cheese. My mum likes cheese.

M: You've got bread and cheese?

W: Yes. That's it!

2

M1: What's the weather like today, Harry?

M2: It's nice. There are clouds in the sky and it isn't windy.

M1: Is it rainy?

M2: No. It isn't rainy and it isn't sunny ... it's cloudy and a good day to go for a walk with my dog.

Exam preparation Tests A and B. Test Booklet.
Activity 4. Listen and colour.

1

M: Look. This is a picture of a house and garden. Do you want to colour it?

W: Yes, please.

M: OK. Can you see the bird under the tree?

W: Yes.

M: Can you colour that bird green?

W: OK.

2

M: OK. Now ... can you see the bird on the house?

W: On the house ... err ... ah yes!

M: Ok. That bird is blue.

W: Can I colour it blue?

M: Yes. Colour it blue.

W: OK.

3

M: Now look at the car.

W: OK. There's a bird on the car. Do you want me to colour it?

M: Yes, I do.

W: Can I colour it red and yellow?

M: Yes, OK. Colour its head red and its body and tail yellow.

W: OK.

4

M: Look behind the house. Can you see the bird?

W: Yes. What colour is that bird?

M: What colour would you like to colour it?

W: Umm. I'd like to colour it purple and pink.

M: OK. Colour it purple and pink.

W: Like this?

M: Yes. That's right.

5

M: OK. Now ... can you see the bird in the tree?

W: Above the bird under the tree?

M: Yes. That bird. I want you to colour it brown and orange.

W: Can I colour the head orange and the body brown?

M: Yes. That's fine.

Evaluation chart

PUPIL'S NAME	EVALUATION CHART								
	Placement	1	2	3	4	5	6	7	8

MARKING CRITERIA: ★ = Still developing   ★★ = Progressing well   ★★★ = Excellent

Evaluation chart

PUPIL'S NAME	End of term 1	End of term 2	End of term 3	Final	Exam preparation

MARKING CRITERIA: ★ = Still developing ★★ = Progressing well ★★★ = Excellent

Pearson Education Limited
Edinburgh Gate
Harlow
Essex CM20 2JE
England
and Associated Companies throughout the world.

Poptropica® English Islands

First published 2017
Second impression 2017
ISBN: 978-1-2921-9838-5

Set in Fiendstar 12/14pt
Printed in Neografia, Slovakia

Acknowledgements: The publisher would like to thank Kerry Powell and
Katie Foufouti for their contributions to this edition.

Illustrators: Chan Sui Fai, Adam Clay, Moreno Chiacchiera (Beehive
Illustration), Tom Heard (The Bright Agency), Andrew Hennessey, Marek
Jagucki, Sue King (Plum Pudding Illustration), Stephanine Lau, Katie
McDee, Bill McGuire (Shannon Associates), Jackie Stafford, Olimpia Wong
and Yam Wai Lun

All other images © Pearson Education

Every effort has been made to trace the copyright holders and we
apologize in advance for any unintentional omissions. We would be
pleased to insert the appropriate acknowledgement in any subsequent
edition of this publication.

ISBN 978-1-292-19838-5